Pebble® Plus

because

and

or

What Is a CONJUNCTION?

so

but

by Jennifer Fandel

Consulting Editor: Gail Saunders-Smith, PhD

PARTS OF SPEECH

CAPSTONE PRESS
a capstone imprint

Pebble Plus is published by Capstone Press,
1710 Roe Crest Drive, North Mankato, Minnesota 56003.
www.capstonepub.com

Library of Congress Cataloging-in-Publication Data
Cataloging-in-publication information is on file with the Library of Congress.
ISBN 978-1-62065-130-8 (library binding)
ISBN 978-1-4765-1729-2 (eBook PDF)

Editorial Credits
Jill Kalz, editor; Heidi Thompson, designer; Marcie Spence, media researcher; Laura Manthe, production specialist

Photo Credits
Alamy Images: Enigma, 21, Jim West, 17, William Manning, 9; iStockphotos: pick-uppath, 11; Shutterstock: Andy Dean Photography, cover (boy), ARENA Creative, 7, Cathelion C, 19, DenisNata, cover (girl), Distinctive Images, 5, Dominic Laniewicz, 15, Hayati Kayhan, cover (pencils), MSPhotographic, 13, OKSun, cover (girl with present), YanLev, 6

Note to Parents and Teachers

The Parts of Speech set supports English language arts standards related to grammar. This book describes and illustrates conjunctions. The images support early readers in understanding the text. The repetition of words and phrases helps early readers learn new words. This book also introduces early readers to subject-specific vocabulary words, which are defined in the Glossary section. Early readers may need assistance to read some words and to use the Table of Contents, Glossary, Read More, Internet Sites, and Index sections of the book.

Printed in the United States of America in North Mankato, Minnesota.
092012   006933CGS13

Table of Contents

Meet the Conjunctions

A conjunction is one part of speech. It joins words and sentences together. These words are common conjunctions: and, but, or, because, so.

and

and

and

The word "and"
is used for adding.
The word "but"
is a way to show
what is different.

Tommy <u>and</u> Renee
walk to school.

Scout likes the swimming pool <u>but</u> not the bathtub.

The word "or" shows choices.

Something can be one way

or the other.

It cannot be both.

Will the red car <u>or</u> the yellow car win the race?

The word "because" shows
a reason. The word "so"
shows a purpose. Both words
answer the question, "Why?"

Travis wears a cape <u>because</u> he is a superhero.

Please get down <u>so</u> you don't hurt yourself.

11

Finding Conjunctions

A conjunction may be found

almost anywhere in a sentence.

It may be at the start.

But it's never at the end.

But I like cheese and ham on my sandwich.

13

A conjunction often joins
two or more of the same parts
of speech. Nouns go with
nouns. Verbs go with verbs.
Adjectives go with adjectives.

Dolphins **and** their young swim in the ocean.
noun   noun

They jump **and** splash.
verb   verb

They are gray, white, **or** black.
adjective adjective   adjective

15

More and More!

A conjunction often ties
two sentences together.
It connects two
complete thoughts.

Alex hits a home run,
and the crowd cheers.

When a conjunction joins
two sentences, it has a helper.
A comma goes before
the conjunction.

The dog woke, but the cat slept.

comma

Conjunctions are like glue. They make words *and* sentences stick together.

Glossary

adjective—a word that gives details about a noun

comma—a punctuation mark used to separate words, groups of words, or numbers

noun—a word that names a person, place, or object

purpose—the reason for doing or making something

verb—a word used to express action or state of being

Read More

Ganeri, Anita. *Joining Words: Conjunctions.* Getting to Grips with Grammar. Chicago: Heinemann Library, 2012.

Loewen, Nancy. *If You Were a Conjunction.* Word Fun. Minneapolis: Picture Window Books, 2007.

Walton, Rick. *Just Me and 6,000 Rats: An Adventure in Conjunctions.* Layton, Utah: Gibbs Smith, 2011.

Internet Sites

FactHound offers a safe, fun way to find Internet sites related to this book. All of the sites on FactHound have been researched by our staff.

Here's all you do:

Visit *www.facthound.com*

Type in this code: 9781620651308

Super-cool stuff!
Check out projects, games and lots more at
www.capstonekids.com

23

Index

Word Count: 162
Grade: 1
Early-Intervention Level: 23

24